GODS
OF
ANCIENT EGYPT

BRUCE LAFONTAINE

Dover Publications, Inc.
Mineola, New York

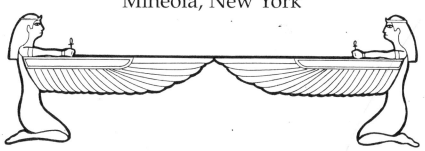

Bibliographical Note

Gods of Ancient Egypt is a new work, first published by Dover Publications, Inc., in 2002.

DOVER *Pictorial Archive* SERIES

International Standard Book Number: 0-486-42088-4

Manufactured in the United States of America
Dover Publications, Inc., 31 East 2nd Street, Mineola, N.Y. 11501

NOTE

The great civilization of ancient Egypt lasted for over 3,000 years as the primary political, military, and cultural power of the Mediterranean and North African region. This civilization was built (as is the modern country of Egypt) around the life-giving waters of the Nile River, the only major river in the world that flows from south to north. The Nile's headwaters are in East and Central Africa. The river flows northward through several modern states into the area known as Upper (southern) Egypt, then enters Lower (northern) Egypt with its broad flood plain, the delta, and eventually empties into the Mediterranean Sea.

There were several eras in the history of ancient Egypt. These were the periods of the Old Kingdom, the Middle Kingdom, and the New Kingdom. In all these periods, hereditary dynasties ruled the land. The kings were called pharaohs and in the official Egyptian religion were considered living embodiments of the gods. They were revered by the people and ruled with absolute power. The connection among the gods, the pharaohs, and the common people was central to Egyptian religion and life.

Ancient Egyptian religion was centered on the idea of birth, death, and rebirth in the afterlife, just as daily life centered on the annual flooding and recession of the waters of the Nile. From this idea came the Egyptian pantheon of many gods who guided and protected various aspects of nature and human existence. Initially, Upper and Lower Egypt each had its own local gods. In Upper Egypt, whose capitol was Heliopolis, the god Atum was considered the supreme deity. In Memphis, part of Lower Egypt, the god Ptah was the chief deity. As Egypt grew and was unified over time into a single kingdom, the local gods were combined into a central set of mythical beings.

The gods were most often represented as human figures with the heads of sacred symbolic animals such as the falcon, bull, ibis, jackal, or crocodile, or as such an animal wearing a royal crown. Each god was associated with a different animal. The falcon and the crocodile both symbolized the majesty and power of the Pharaoh. Each god and its animal had powers and domain over a specific area of Egyptian life.

The idea of death and rebirth into an afterlife was a powerful, pervasive belief for the Egyptians. Many of the ancient artifacts that remain today are associated with this aspect of Egyptian religion. Pyramids and obelisks and the ritual purification and mummification of the body are all reflections of the importance of the afterlife. Several major gods, Osiris and Anubis for example, were primarily associated with life in the underworld, rather than earthly existence.

For only one short period during the thousands of years of ancient Egyptian history did the idea of a single supreme god become a tenet of the official state religion. Pharaoh Amenhotep IV (who reigned from 1379 to 1334 BC) decreed that Aten, represented by the life-giving sun disk, was the only divine creator and ruler of the universe. The Egyptians never accepted this idea, and reverted to their traditional beliefs after the death of Amenhotep. But the concept was a predecessor to later monotheistic religions such as Christianity, Judaism, and Islam, with their shared belief in a single supreme being.

Gods of Ancient Egypt depicts many of the major and minor deities who guided the lives of the ancient Egyptians during the 3,000-year history of their great civilization. Also pictured are various symbols and decorative design motifs from painting, sculpture, and architecture that reflect the dynamic culture of ancient Egypt.

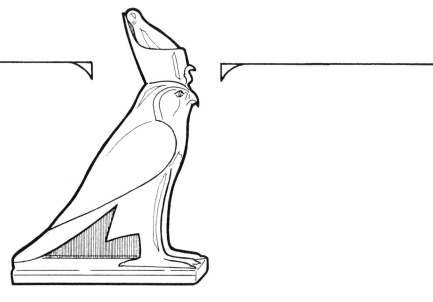

1. *Ra-Atum* with *Shu, Geb, Nut, and Tefnut*

The priests of the ancient city of Heliopolis ("City of the Sun" in Greek) in Lower Egypt believed that the world was created by the sun god Ra. Ra was pictured as a falcon with a sun-disk crown, riding in a papyrus reed boat. The Heliopolitan creation myth described this god gathering himself together from the waters of chaos into the form of a human being.

In Upper Egypt, the people worshipped the god Atum as the creator. His name means "the all" and he was believed to contain the essence of both male and female. When Upper and Lower Egypt were unified into a single kingdom around 1570 BC, the two gods were combined into Ra-Atum, shown on the opposite page. The symbolic falcon illustrated above is wearing the double crown representing Upper and Lower Egypt.

Shown below Ra-Atum are his children and grandchildren. These gods were created from the tears of the great creator. At the far left is Shu, son of Ra-Atum and god of air and light. At far right is Tefnut, goddess of dew and rain, the daughter of Ra-Atum. The children of Shu and Tefnut are shown side by side. They are Geb, god of the earth, and Nut, goddess of the night sky.

The ancient Egyptian system of writing is called hieroglyphics, because it used pictorial symbols called hieroglyphs. These symbols represented sounds, individual people, animals, and objects. Common hierogylyphs appear in the band at the bottom of each right-hand page in this book.

On the opposite page, a cartouche containing the hieroglyphic symbols for Ra-Atum is depicted below his boat. (A cartouche is an oval frame; the ancient Egyptians used it in their hieroglyphic writing to set off or display the symbols or seals of the gods and of royalty.)

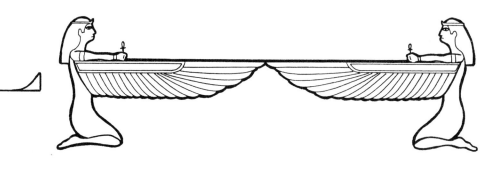

2. *Amun-Ra*

Amun-Ra (also spelled Amen- or Amon-Re) became the chief national god of Egypt when Upper and Lower Egypt were united during the XVIIIth dynasty (approximately 1570 BC). Originally, Amun was the wind god of the city of Thebes in Lower Egypt and Ra or Re was the widely recognized sun god. Egyptians believed that human beings were created by the tears of Ra. On the opposite page, Amun is shown wearing a traditional tall feathered crown, while Ra is depicted with the head of a falcon wearing a sun disc and cobra crown. Both gods are pictured holding an ankh, the looped cross that was the Egyptian symbol of life.

In this illustration, the hieroglyphic symbols for Amun and Ra appear in cartouches above their heads. Other common hieroglyphs appear in the cartouche designs at the bottom of this page as well as in the band at the bottom of the facing page.

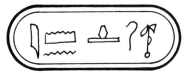

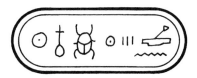

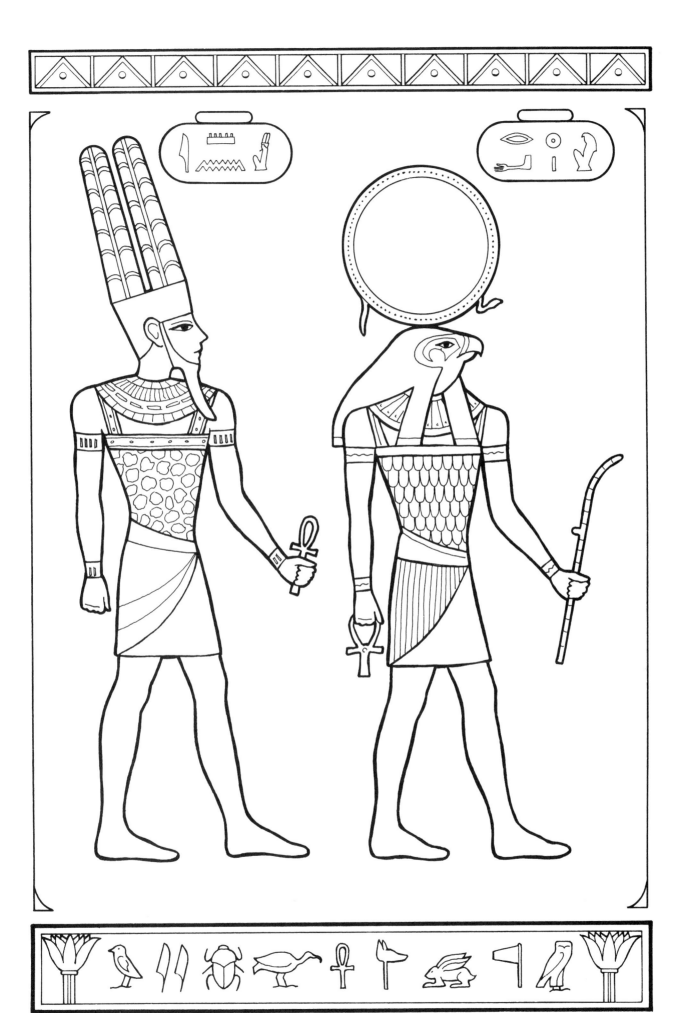

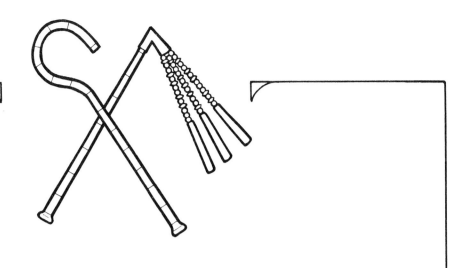

3. *Osiris*

One of the chief gods of ancient Egypt, Osiris was the first child of Geb and Nut. He was the god of fertility and farming and revealed the stories of the gods to the Egyptian priests. Osiris was killed by his jealous brother Seth (Set), who trapped him in a gilded coffin and threw the coffin into the Nile. His body was recovered by his grieving wife Isis. Seth discovered this and, in his rage, cut Osiris' body into pieces and scattered them throughout Egypt. Isis eventually collected these remains and restored the body through her mystical powers. Osiris then became the god of the underworld, judging the dead as they entered his kingdom.

Osiris is always shown with green skin, symbolizing life and rebirth. He is depicted holding the crook and flail, symbols of power of the Pharaohs. The crook was a badge of royal authority and the flail symbolized the fertility of the land.

Here Osiris is pictured with a royal sarcophagus on either side. A sarcophagus was an elaborately carved, painted, and gilded coffin used to help preserve the mummified bodies of members of the Pharaoh's family and of the royal court.

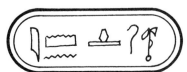
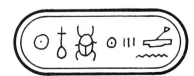

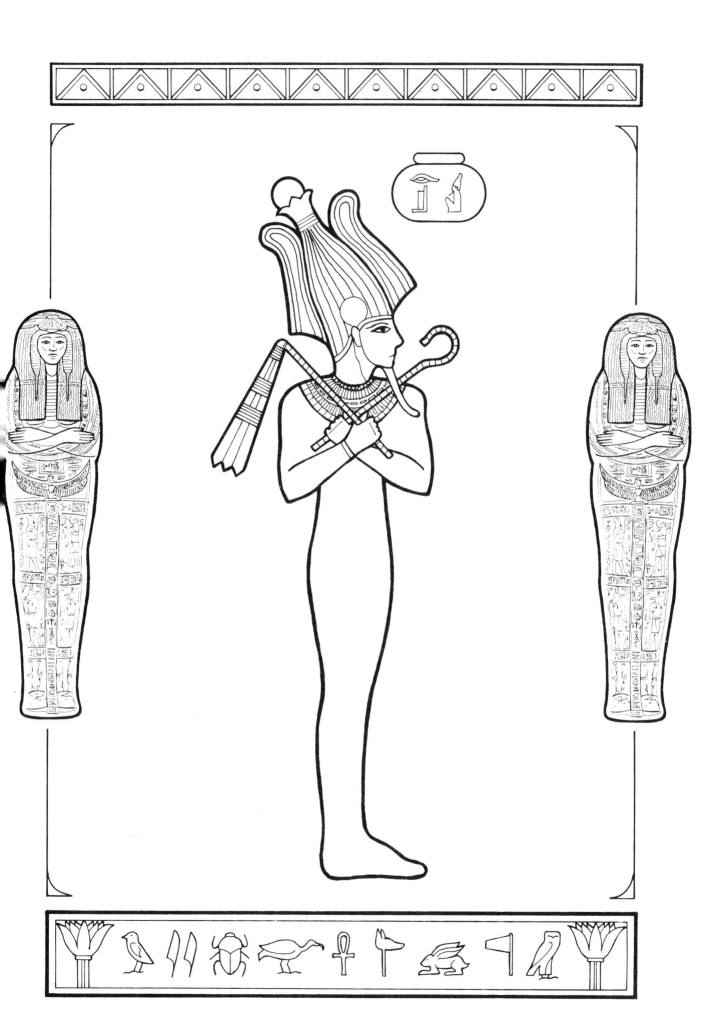

4. *Isis*

The goddess Isis was the wife and sister of Osiris (such marriages were common among ancient Egyptian royalty). She was the goddess of love, motherhood, destiny, and magic. The Egyptians believed that the Nile was created from her tears. This made her a symbol of the fertility of the land watered by the sacred Nile. Isis was the mother of Horus, the falcon-headed god of the rising sun. She is depicted opposite wearing a crown of bull horns surrounding a sun disk and holding a jackal-headed royal scepter. Isis was also commonly pictured wearing a royal throne as a crown. After the decline of the Egyptian civilization, Isis became one of the prominent deities of the Roman world.

Shown above is a necklace called a pectoral. Worn around the neck and over the shoulders, it was a decorative accessory often worn by royalty and other prominent Egyptians. Integrated into the design of this pectoral are many common Egyptian symbols, including the falcon wings of the god Horus, the all-seeing "Eye of Horus," a winged scarab (sacred beetle) insignia, cobra symbols, the sun disk, and stylized plant forms (lotus buds).

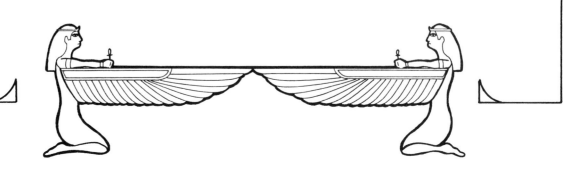

5. *Horus*

The sky god Horus was represented as either a falcon or as a man with the head of a falcon. He was the son of Isis and Osiris and nephew of Seth. According to Egyptian mythology, Horus and Seth had many battles to determine who would be king of the gods. When his evil uncle had Horus' eyes put out, the world was plunged into darkness. He was healed after the goddess Hathor poured milk into his eyes. Osiris eventually intervened from the underworld and proclaimed Horus the chief deity of the Egyptians. The god Horus became the symbolic protector of the living pharaoh. Shown above is the all-seeing "Eye of Horus," a symbolic decoration commonly used in Egyptian sculpture, jewelry, and painting.

On the opposite page Horus is depicted wearing the double crown that represented both Upper and Lower Egypt. The lower part of the crown was red and the upper portion white. The god is pictured with an obelisk on each side. (An obelisk is a free-standing, four-sided, tapered rectangular stone pillar capped with a pyramid shape.) Obelisks were erected throughout the kingdom to commemorate great pharaohs and their achievements.

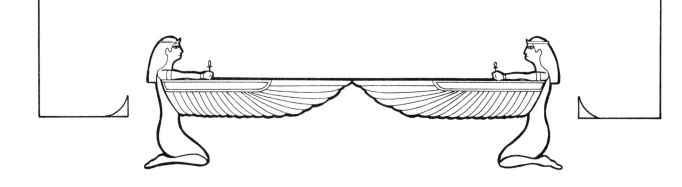

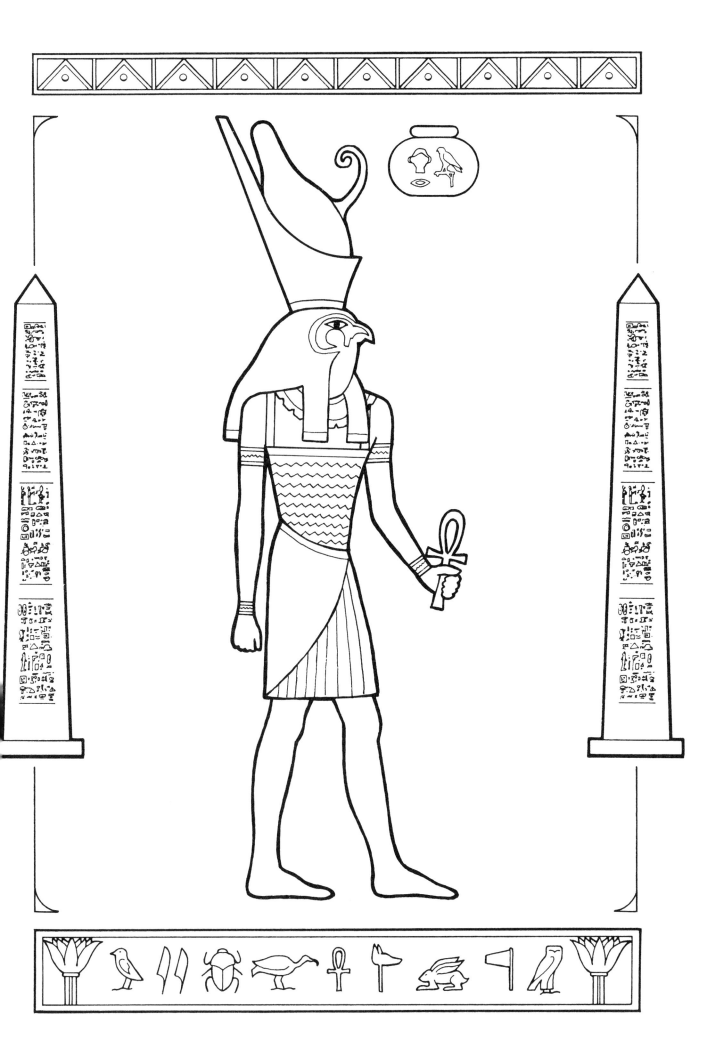

6. *Seth* (*Set*)

The great enemy of Osiris and Horus, the god Seth symbolized darkness and evil. He is represented on the facing page with the head of a ram. His eyes and hair were red, a color Egyptians associated with evil. Seth was also depicted as a pig, a serpent, and a hippopotamus. After he was defeated in his quest to become king of the gods, the sun god Ra made him god of storms and chaos. He was exiled to rule in the kingdom of the barren Egyptian desert.

Shown above is a symbol of the sacred scarab beetle. It was widely used in many forms for decoration and as a seal of authority. The scarab was depicted with wings both folded and outstretched, as in the stylized version above.

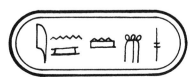

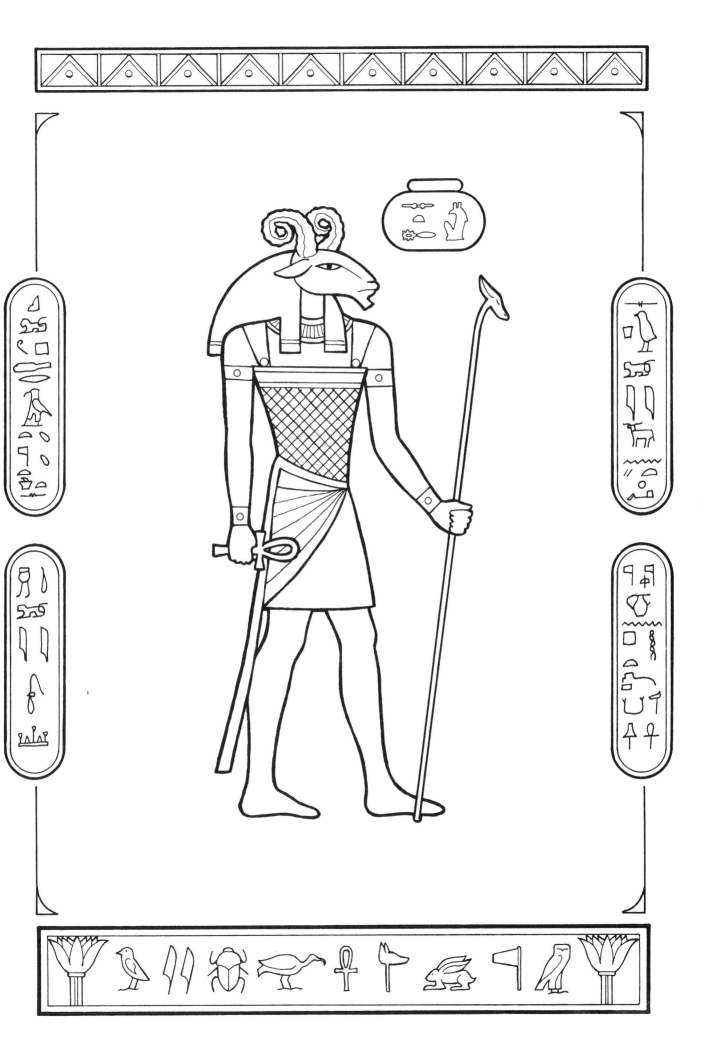

7. Hathor

Hathor was the daughter of Ra and Nut. She was the goddess of love and fertility and protector of women. She also provided food and water to the souls of the dead on their journey to the underworld. Her sacred animal was the cow and she is depicted wearing a crown of cow horns surrounding a sun disk and holding a lotus blossom scepter. She was the wife of the sky god Horus and her life-giving milk healed his eyes after they were plucked out by the evil Seth. When the sun god Ra sent her to destroy mortal human beings, she was transformed into Sekhmet, goddess of war.

Flanking the illustration of Hathor are two classic Egyptian stone columns. The ancient Egyptians were extremely skilled at cutting, carving, and assembling huge blocks of stone to build their many palaces, monuments, and temples. One of the few remaining buildings from the great Egyptian age is the Temple at Karnak. The main hall of this structure is lined with limestone columns over 75 feet high. These support pillars end in elaborately shaped capitals, many carved in the design of stylized plant forms such as the papyrus reed or the lotus flower.

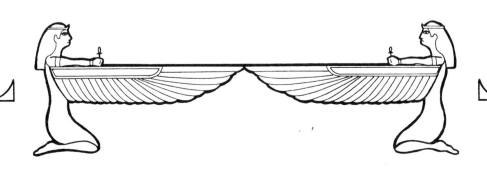

8. *Anubis*

With his jackal's head, the god Anubis is probably one of the most recognizable of the ancient Egyptian deities. He was the god of funerals and mummification, two very important rites in the Egyptian religion. When his father Osiris was murdered by Seth, Anubis wrapped and preserved his body, creating the first mummy. He served in the underworld with Osiris as the judge of the entering dead, weighing their hearts to determine the amount of good and evil done during each person's life. Shown on either side of Anubis are examples of royal sarcophagi representing his role as god of funeral rites.

   Shown above is a gold, enamel, and glass necklace pendant in the shape of the vulture goddess Nekhbet. She was protector of the pharaoh and his royal children.

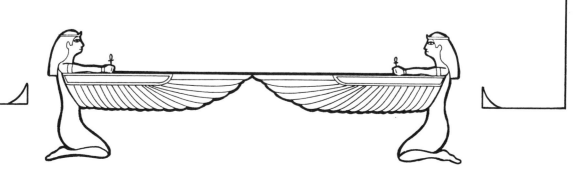

9. *Thoth*

Depicted with the head of an ibis (a water bird), Thoth was the god of the moon and of wisdom. His myth credits him with inventing many intellectual pursuits, including writing, astronomy, geometry, magic, medicine, and music. One of his tasks was to write the names of dead souls as they entered the underworld. He is pictured on the opposite page with a papyrus scroll and writing implement. The hieroglyphic cartouche for Thoth is shown next to him and he is flanked by elaborately carved and painted obelisks.

Shown below on this page are two winged female figures. Both male and female figures with stylized bird wings were a popular design motif in ancient Egypt. These winged female forms are suggestive of the goddess Ma'at.

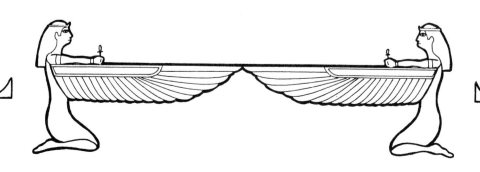

10. *Bes*

The god Bes was represented by the figure of a misshapen dwarf.
The Egyptians believed that ugly creatures could frighten away evil
spirits. Bes protected the family and was the god of luck, dancing,
music, and feasting. He is often shown with a tambourine or harp.
Bes was a popular god with the common people of ancient Egypt,
and many carved figurines of him were created.

Shown above on this page is another common decorative symbol,
the all-seeing "Eye of Horus." The illustration depicts a necklace
pendant made with gold, enamel, and glass. Egyptian artisans were
very skilled at working and molding soft metals such as gold, cop-
per, and silver. They were also masters at cutting and using gems
such as rubies and sapphires, and semiprecious minerals such as
turquoise, in the creation of finely wrought jewelry.

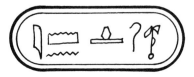

11. *Bastet*

The goddess Bastet was the daughter of Ra, the sun god. She was worshipped as the goddess of sexuality and childbirth and was considered the bringer of sunlight to the Earth. She is represented on the facing page with the head of a cat. Egyptians revered the cat as a sacred animal and often mummified cats to honor Bastet. Cats were kept as pets, and statues of cats were commonplace, in both royal palaces and workmen's mud huts.

Bastet is shown with her hieroglyphic cartouche and is flanked by carved stone columns.

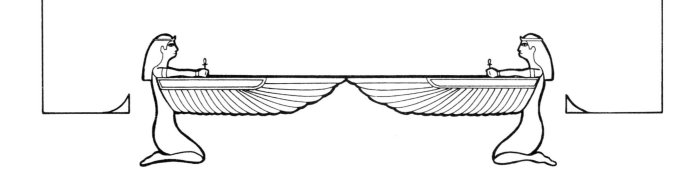

12. *Sobek*

Nile crocodiles were feared and admired for their speed and strength and were one of the symbols of the Pharaoh's power. The crocodile-headed god Sobek had many temples dedicated to him in the Nile valley (including his chief temple at Crocodilopolis), and continued to be worshipped into the era of the Greeks and Romans. Here he is depicted carrying a jackal-headed staff of authority and wearing a crown of tall feathers, cobras, and a sun disk. He is flanked on either side by monumental stone obelisks. His symbolic cartouche appears near his crocodile head.

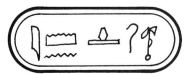 

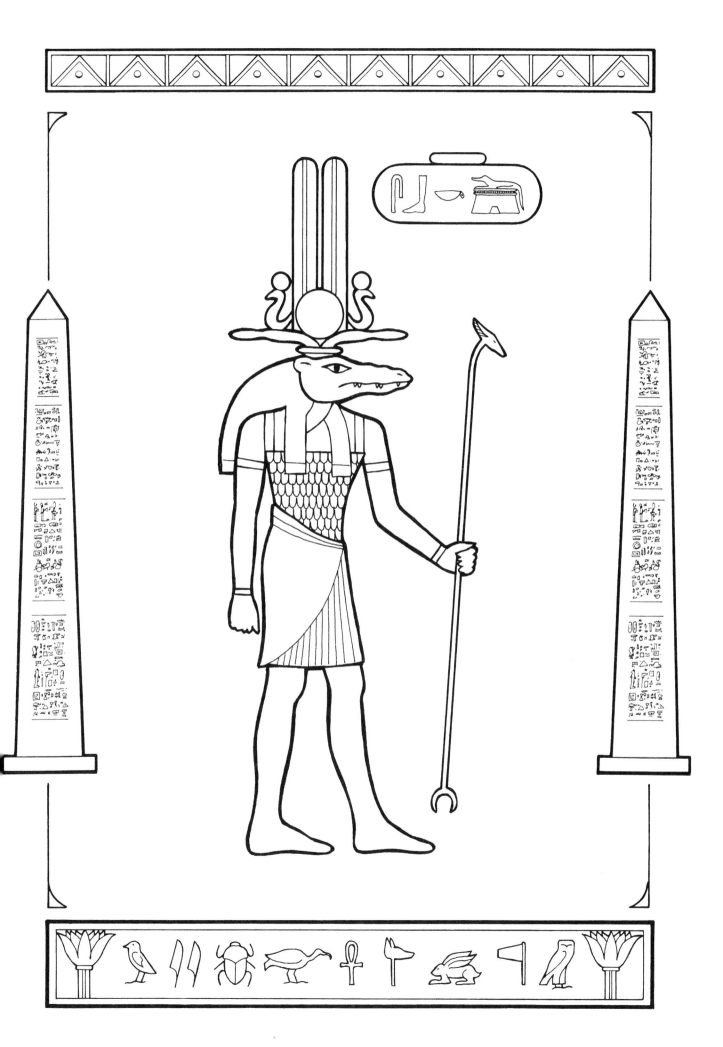

13. *Taweret*

One of the Egyptians many animal-form deities, Taweret was the goddess who protected women during childbirth. She is depicted on the facing page with the head of a hippopotamus, the tail of a crocodile, and the body of a lion. Her fearsome appearance was thought to frighten away evil spirits during birth. Pregnant women would wear a charm around their necks with the figure of Taweret for protection. Pictured on either side of the goddess are stone columns with capitals carved in the shape of lotus petals. Shown above on this page is a symbolic representation of Ra, the sun god, enclosed within the classic pyramid shape.

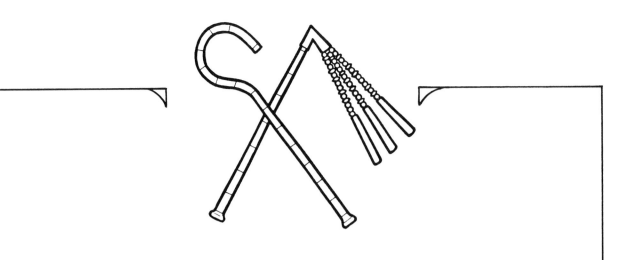

14. *Aten* with Nefertiti and Akhenaten

During the New Kingdom reign of the Pharaoh Amenhotep IV, around 1350 BC, the official state religion of Egypt was altered from the traditional pantheistic ("of many gods") worship to a monotheistic worship of a single supreme deity. Amenhotep banned worship of the other gods in favor of Aten, represented by the Sun disk, as the sole creator and ruler of the world. The Pharaoh even changed his name to Akhenaten, meaning "beloved of Aten," and moved his capitol city from Thebes to the site of the temple erected to Aten at Tel el-Amarna. Aten is shown above as a sun disk with rays ending in hands holding the sacred symbol of life, the Ankh.

Akhenaten's principal wife was Nefertiti, shown here with the Pharaoh. One of the most famous artifacts of ancient Egypt is a bust of this queen. This sculpture has for centuries been regarded as a representation of an ideal feminine beauty, a depiction of one of the most beautiful women who ever lived.

After the death of Akhenaten, Egypt reverted back to its traditional worship of many gods. Akhenaten was reviled as a heretic and many of the statues and paintings representing him were destroyed.

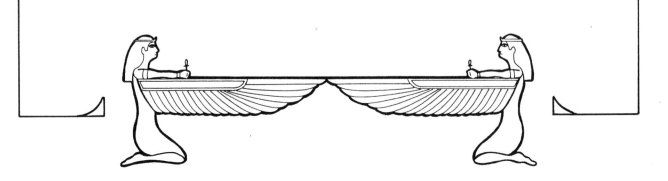